Spiralizer Coo[...] delicious Easy Spiralizer Recipies

By Salutem Tunnel

Table of Contents

Introduction

Having a spiralizer can open up a host of new and creative ways to prepare food especially vegetables. Do you own a spiralizer? Are you interested in mouthwatering recipes that you can use your spiralizer to prepare? Have you ever wanted a way to prepare low carb meals without it being boring or tasteless? Well look no further because you have just found the ultimate spiralizer recipe book.

This book contains 90+ incredible, tantalizing recipes that just about anyone can prepare. You will never be bored with your spiralizer with this cookbook in your collection. Soon you will be preparing just about everything with your spiralizer. Having a spiralizer in your kitchen can make chopping vegetables and fruits a thing of the past. Now you can turn your fruits and veggies into eye-catching spirals, noodles and ribbons.

Having a hard time getting the kids to eat their veggies? Turn plain old vegetables into eye-catching spirals that will have you and your family eating healthy in no time. You simply can't go wrong with this spiralizer recipe book. Enjoy making these meals for breakfast, lunch and dinner and see just how much you can make using your spiralizer.

From simple salads to soups and desserts and everything in between. You will enjoy each and every creation that you prepare. Bet you never imagined making pancakes, pizza or pudding using your spiralizer. The spiralizing experience will be an interesting one with you making dishes such as:

CREAMY CAULIFLOWER, CHICK PEAS CHICKEN NOODLES

POTATO ALFREDO

SPIRALIZED PANCAKES

CARROT AND NUTMEG PUDDING

You can make these and so much more. Each dish low in carbs and freshly made so you know exactly what you are putting into each meal. Go ahead, grab your spiralizer and let's get spiralized!! **Happy Cooking!**

Curly Beetroot Salad topped with Goat Cheese & Almond Dressing

Have a healthy start to your day with this fun curly beetroot salad, topped with creamy, sweet almond dressing and goat cheese for added tang

Servings: 3

Preparation Time: 30 minutes

Ingredients

- Sea Salt (1/4 teaspoon)

- Honey (1/2 teaspoon)

- Lemon Juice (2 tablespoons)

- Olive Oil (1/4 cup)

- Garlic (1 clove, minced)

- Almonds (1/4 Cup)

- Large Carrot (1)

- Large Beets (2)

- Goat Cheese (5 slices)

Directions

1. Clean and prepare the beetroots and carrot

2. Use spiralizer to create noodles from the beetroots and carrot.

3. Add sea salt, honey, lemon juice, olive oil, garlic and almonds to a food processor or a blender and combine until slightly smooth.

4. Combine the beetroot and carrot noodles with the dressing and sprinkle with goat cheese.

5. Serve and Enjoy

Radish & Chicken Sesame Salad

This amazing Asian delight combines flavors from crunchy radish and succulent chicken breast to deliver a memorable salad

Servings: 1

Preparation Time: 20 minutes

Ingredients

- Olive Oil (1 tablespoon)

- Lime Juice (1 tablespoon)

- Soy Sauce (1 tablespoon)

- Honey (1/2 tablespoon)

- Coconut Oil (1 tablespoon)

- Onion (1/2, diced)

- Garlic (1 clove, minced)

- Ginger (1, grated)

- Sesame Seeds (1 tablespoon)

- 3 Radishes (Peeled)

- 2 Chicken Breast (Grilled)

- 4 ribbons Dulse (chopped)

Directions

1. Cook Sesame seeds in a small pan until lightly brown and set aside to cool

2. Leave Dulse in cold water for 3 minutes, then cut in small pieces

3. Prepare dressing in a bowl using soy sauce, lime juice, honey and olive oil.

4. Prepare radishes into noodles using desired blade in your spiralizer.

5. Mix grilled chicken breast, sesame seeds, dulse and radish noodles together.

6. Pour dressing and serve

Celeriac Pasta with Lemon and Apple Sauce

The rich taste of celeriac goes well with the sweetness of apple and fragrant hazelnut oil.

Servings: 1

Preparation Time: 15 minutes

Ingredients

- Apple (1, sliced)

- Lemon Juice (2 tablespoon)

- Honey (1 teaspoon)

- Black Pepper (1 teaspoon)

- Green Onion (1, diced)

- Celeriac (1)

- Fresh Thyme

Directions

1. Clean and prepare celeriac to be used in a spiralizer. Fit spiralizer with desired blade and process celeriac into noodles.

2. Toss created noodles in lemon juice and set aside

3. Prepare the sauce by combining apple, lemon juice, honey, black pepper and green onion in a bowl.

4. Combine noodles with sauce and serve topped with fresh thyme.

Rich Cucumber Noodles

Bring some Greek flavor to your plate with these cucumber noodles. Go ahead and topped with your favorites and enjoy.

Servings: 4

Preparation Time: 15 minutes

Ingredients

- Plain Hummus- brand of your choose (4 tablespoons)

- Red onion (1/2, sliced)

- Kalamata Olives (1/2 cup, pitted, chopped)

- Feta Cheese (1/2, crushed)

- Grape Tomatoes (1 cup, halved)

- Cucumbers (2)

Directions

1. Prepare the cucumber to be used in the spiralizer to create the noodles. Fit spiralizer with desired blade and process cucumber into noodles.

2. Plate the noodles and top with hummus, red onions, olives and tomatoes

3. Sprinkle with feta cheese, salt and pepper

4. Serve and Enjoy

Carrot Noodle Salad with Ginger-Lemon Peanut Sauce

There is just no denying how fabulous this raw dish is, you can't help but try to create it for yourself.

Serving: 6

Preparation Time: 15 minutes

Ingredients

- Lemon Juice (1 tablespoon)

- Coconut Milk (4 tablespoons)

- Peanut Butter (2 tablespoons)

- Large Garlic (2 cloves, diced)

- Ginger (1, grated)

- Large Carrots (5, peeled)

- Roasted Almonds (1/3 cup)

- Cilantro (2 tablespoons, sliced finely)

Directions

1. Place peeled carrots in spiralizer to create noodles

2. In a bowl mix lemon juice, coconut milk, peanut butter, garlic and ginger until texture is smooth and creamy

3. Plate carrots noodles and pour mixture on combine until all noodles are coated

4. Sprinkle with almonds, cilantro and serve.

Creamy Cauliflower, Chick Peas Chicken Noodles

Cauliflower Noodles? Yes, once you get the hang of it using your trusty spiralizer you will be in love with this dish.

Servings: 3

Preparation Time: 35 minutes

Ingredients

- Cauliflower Stems (3)

- Chicken Breast (2)

- Canned Chickpeas (1/2 cup, washed and drained)

- Leeks (1/2 cup, sliced)

- Olive Oil (2 tablespoon)

- Oregano Flakes (1/4 teaspoon)

- Shallot (1/2, sliced)

- Garlic (1 clove, crushed)

- Basil (2 tablespoons, sliced)

- Feta (1/4 cup)

- Lemon Juice (1 tablespoon)

- Red wine vinegar (1 tablespoon)

Directions

1. Season chicken breast with salt, pepper and oregano on both sides and fry in pan over medium heat for 15minutes on both sides.

2. Place the cauliflower stems in spiralizer, once the noodles are created boil for 5 minutes, drain and set aside to cool

3. Combine olive oil, shallot, garlic, basil, lemon juice, red wine vinegar and feta, to create the dressing

4. Plate in the cauliflower noodles, chick peas, leeks and top with dressing

5. Serve and Enjoy.

Zucchini Fettuccine topped with Rosemary-Butternut Sauce

Glazed with rich rosemary and peanut sauce, this zucchini fettuccine is the perfect meal for date night, girls' night or a warm night at home

Servings: 6

Preparation Time: 70 minutes

Ingredients

- Coconut Milk (1 cup)

- Coconut Oil (3 tablespoons)

- Vegetable Broth (1/2 cup)

- Small Onion (1, sliced)

- Garlic (2 cloves, crushed)

- Rosemary (2 teaspoons)

- Zucchini (3lbs)

- Butternut Squash (1)

Directions

1. Set oven to 375 degrees

2. Slice butternut squash in half, grease baking skin with coconut oil and place butternut squash cut side down and roast for 45 minutes

3. Let cool and spoon the flesh out and add to blender

4. In a pan over medium heat sauté onion, garlic and rosemary in coconut oil for 5 minutes

5. Add the sautéed mixture to blender and blend with coconut milk, broth, salt and pepper until texture is smooth

6. Fit spiralizer with blade to create zucchini fettuccine.

7. In the same pan that first mixture was sauté add fettuccine and cook for 2 minutes until tender but not soft.

8. Combine mixture from blender and fettuccine

9. Plate & Serve

Zoodles & Meatballs

So simple, it'll be fun to have the kids involved with this. This is a great way to get them to eat their veggies.

Servings: 4

Preparation Time: 45 minutes

Ingredients

- Zucchini (6)

- Salt (2 tablespoon)

- Black pepper (1 tablespoon)

- Ground Beef (2lbs)

- Bread Crumbs (2 cups)

- Eggs (2)

- Onion (1, crushed)

- Spaghetti Sauce- brand of your choice

Directions

1. Create the noodles by placing the zucchini in the spiralizer and set aside

2. Season ground beef with salt, pepper and onion

3. Roll into balls, dip in egg and then coat in bread crumbs

4. Fry balls in pan over medium heat

5. Plate noodles and balls and pour sauce on top.

6. Serve & Enjoy

Ginger Zucchini Egg Noodle Soup

Easy to make egg teardrop soup, convenient for breakfast or lunch with the touch of fresh zucchini noodles

Servings: 6

Preparation Time: 35 minutes

Ingredients

- Olive Oil (2 tablespoons)

- Ginger (2 tablespoons, crushed)

- Vegetable Broth (8 cups)

- Soy Sauce (5 tablespoons)

- Water (2 cups)

- Scallions (2 cups, sliced)

- Corn Starch (3 tablespoons)

- Red Pepper Flakes (1/2 teaspoons)

- Large Egg (4, beaten)

- Large Zucchini (4)

- Mushrooms (5 cups)

Directions

1. Prepare the zucchini noodles with spiralizer and set it aside

2. Heat olive oil in a pan over medium heat, add crushed ginger and stir in pan for 2 minutes

3. Add mushrooms and tablespoon of water and cook for 2 minutes

4. Pour in 7 cups of broth, tablespoon of water, red pepper flakes, soy sauce and bring to a boil in a separate pan.

5. Combine one cup of broth and corn starch in a different bowl and stir until smooth, then pour this mixture slowly into the soup pot and leave to boil until thickened

6. Add mushroom mixture and then add eggs slowly to the pot and combine slowly until thoroughly incorporated

7. Add zucchini noodles and leave to boil for 2 minutes

8. Serve topped with scallions.

Spiralized Pancakes

Put a spin on breakfast by trying these seasoned pancakes. Not the traditional pancake mix but you won't regret it.

Servings: 20

Preparation Time: 40 minutes

Ingredients

- Flour (1/4 cup)

- Black Pepper (1/2 teaspoon)

- Sea Salt (2 teaspoons)

- Medium Onion (1, sliced)

- Olive Oil (2 tablespoon)

- Eggs (4)

- Gold Potatoes (5, peeled)

Directions

1. Place the potatoes in the spiralizer to get potato strings.

2. Heat olive oil in pan over medium heat.

3. Add flour, salt, black pepper, onion, eggs and potato to a bowl and stir to combine.

4. Create flat pancake shapes and place in pan

5. Fry for 3 minutes on each side

6. Remove from pan and serve immediately.

Sweet Potato Spiral Fries

Fun meal for the kids to assist in making and also enjoy. This is a great alternative to French fries.

Servings: 4

Preparation Time: 45 minutes

Ingredients

- Olive Oil (3 tablespoons)
- Large Sweet Potatoes (2)
- Salt (1 teaspoon)
- Black Pepper (1 teaspoon)

Directions

1. Set oven to 400 degrees

2. Peel, clean and place sweet potatoes in spiralizer

3. Set baking sheet on tray and place the sweet potatoes fries evenly

4. Drizzle with olive oil, salt and black pepper

5. Bake in oven for 40 minutes

6. Remove from oven and serve with dip of your choose.

Coconut Banana Rice Pudding

For a healthy, rich, quick meal to start your morning, this coconut infused rice pudding will hit the spot

Servings: 1

Preparation Time: 15 minutes

Ingredients

- Raisins (1/2 cup)

- Coconut Flakes (2 teaspoon)

- Cinnamon (3 tablespoon)

- Vanilla Almond Milk (1 1/2 cup)

- Large Ripe Plantain (1)

Directions

1. Place plantain in spiralizer to create noodles, place the noodles in a blender and pulse until it has a rice texture.

2. Add one (1) cup of almond milk and plantain rice bits in sauce pan

3. Bring the mixture to a boil, then let simmer for 5 minutes then pour the remaining cup of almond milk and simmer for another 5 minutes

4. Remove mixture from heat and sprinkle with cinnamon, coconut flakes and raisins, mix until cinnamon is complete incorporated.

5. Serve in a bowl & Enjoy.

Sweet Apple Noodles with Cinnamon & Coconut Flakes

Apple and cinnamon can only get better with coconut. The right balance of sweet and spiced goodness.

Servings: 4

Preparation Time: 20 minutes

Ingredients

- Coconut Oil (2 tablespoons)

- Large Apples (4)

- Cinnamon (2 tablespoon)

- Coconut Flakes (1/2 cup)

Directions

1. Place apples in spiralizer to create thin spaghetti.

2. Pour the coconut oil in a pan over medium heat and sauté apple spaghetti until soft

3. Sprinkle cinnamon and mix

4. Plate the spaghetti and sprinkle toasted coconut flakes on top

5. Sweet Tooth Served!!

Sweet Potato Pumpkin Noodle Waffles

Every thought of creating your own southern style sweet potato pie. These delicious waffles replicate just that.

Servings: 2

Preparation Time: 25 minutes

Ingredients

- Pumpkin Spice (2 tablespoons)

- Large Egg (1, whisked)

- Maple Syrup (2 tablespoons)

- Large Sweet Potato (2, skinned)

Directions

1. Set the waffle iron to start warming

2. Place the sweet potato in the spiralizer to create noodles

3. Place sweet potato noodles in medium pan, spray with cooking spray, over high heat for 5 minutes

4. Remove from stove and add to bowl, sprinkle with cinnamon and add egg, mix until fully incorporated

5. Spray the waffle iron and add sweet potato noodles

6. Create waffles based on waffle maker settings

7. Plate and serve with maple syrup.

Zucchini Noodles with Garlic Shrimp & Corn

Create a mixture of sweetness from corn and robust garlic shrimp come together for a mouthwatering experience.

Servings: 4

Preparation Time: 45 minutes

Ingredients

- Medium Onion (1, minced)

- Vegetable Broth (4 cups)

- Garlic (3 cloves, crushed)

- White Wine (1/4 cup)

- Cornstarch (1 tablespoon)

- Kernel Corn (2 cups)

- Medium Shrimp (1lb, deveined and sliced in half)

- Zucchini (4lbs, small)

- Salt & Pepper to taste

Directions

Spiralizer Recipes

1. In a pan over medium heat, sauté onion for four (4) minutes

2. Place zucchini in spiralizer to create noodles, rinse and add to pan with onions

3. Once zucchini started to brown add the corn, ½ cup of vegetable broth, salt and pepper

4. Lower the heat and simmer for five (5) minutes

5. In another pan, bring a frying pan to high heat, add garlic and shrimp mix for three (3) minutes, pour wine and sauté for one (1) minute

6. Add this mixture to the noodles

7. Combine the remaining vegetable broth with cornstarch the pour over shrimp mixture

8. Leave on stove until sauce thickens

9. Plate and Serve.

Chicken Taco Zucchini Noodles

Tacos and Zucchini Noodles- weird but amazing pair

Servings: 2

Preparation Time: 20 minutes

Ingredients

- Red Onion (1/4 cup, sliced)

- Tomatoes (2, sliced and seeds removed)

- Black Beans (1/3 cup)

- Red Pepper Flakes (1 teaspoon)

- Garlic (1 clove, crushed)

- Oregano Flakes (1 teaspoon)

- Olive Oil (1 1/2 tablespoon)

- Black Olives (1/2 cup, halved)

- Queso fresco (1/3, crumbled)

- Cilantro (2 tablespoons)

- Avocado (1, diced)

- Chicken Broth (1/4 cup)

- Chicken Breast (2, shredded)

- Zucchini (3)

- Salt & Pepper to taste

Directions

1. Add oil to pan and heat over medium flame.

2. Add garlic, red pepper flakes and onions and cook until fragrant, about 3 minutes.

3. In the same pan place the shredded chicken and top with oregano.

4. Pour in chicken broth and let it cook until liquid has evaporated, put in tomatoes and cilantro, combine and cook for two (2) minutes.

5. Place zucchini in spiralizer to create noodles.

6. Add avocado, beans, olives and zucchini noodles to pan.

7. Cook until noodles have soften

8. Plate with queso fresco sprinkle on top.

Sweet Potato Noodles, Ham & Vegetable Hash

Switch it up from plain potato because this sweet potato is everything.

Servings: 1

Preparation Time: 30 minutes

Ingredients

- Olive Oil (2 tablespoons)

- Red Bell Pepper (1/2, sliced)

- Red Onion (1/2, sliced)

- Mushrooms (6)

- Garlic Powder (1 teaspoon)

- Chili Powder (1 teaspoon)

- Oregano (1 teaspoon)

- Bacon (2 strips)

- Sweet Potato (1, peeled)

- Parmesan Cheese (1 teaspoon)

Directions

1. Place the peeled sweet potato in spiralizer to create noodles

2. Sauté the strips of bacon in a small frying pan on high heat until crisp.

3. Remove from pan, chop into pieces and set aside to cool

4. In a medium frying pan bring 1 tablespoon of olive oil to heat

5. Add the noodles, garlic powder, salt and pepper

6. Stir and cook until noodles are softened.

7. In another pot over medium heat sauté in olive oil, crushed garlic, red onions, sliced peppers, oregano, chili powder and black pepper, stir for two (2) minutes then add mushrooms and stir for three (3) minutes.

8. Plate noodles and top with mushroom mixture and bacon crisps.

Garlic Ginger Zucchini Noodles with Salmon & Cabbage

Add your noodles to this ginger garlic infused soup. The added cabbage and salmon complete the meal.

Servings: 2

Preparation Time: 30 minutes

Ingredients

- Soy Sauce (1 tablespoon)

- Vegetable Broth (1 cup)

- Ginger (1, grated)

- Garlic (1, crushed)

- Sesame Oil (2 teaspoons)

- Olive Oil (1/2 tablespoon)

- Scallions (1/4 cup)

- 2 heads of Cabbage

- Salmon (2oz, skinless)

- Zucchini (2, peeled)

Directions

1. Place Zucchini in spiralizer to create spaghetti, set aside

2. Cook as Salmon preferred (grill, sautéed, baked or steam)

3. Heat olive oil medium heat in medium pan, add garlic

4. Remove leaves from head of cabbage and slice in halves season with salt and pepper, add to pan and cook for three (3) minutes

5. Pour sesame oil, vegetable broth and soy sauce into pan and mix for one (1) minute

6. Add zucchini noodles and let it cook for five (5) minutes

7. Pour mixture into a bowl and top with green onions

8. Serve & Enjoy.

Potato Pizza

Pizza lovers, it's okay you can have fun with the spiralizer too

Servings: 1 Pizza

Preparation Time: 60 minutes

Ingredients

- Garlic Powder (4 teaspoons)

- Mozzarella Cheese (5 slices)

- Eggs (2)

- Olive Oil (2 tablespoons)

- Basil Leaves (5)

- Tomato Basil sauce (1 cup)

- Potatoes (2)

Directions

1. Place potatoes in spiralizer to create noodles.

2. Pour one (1) tablespoon of olive oil in a medium pan over medium heat

3. Cook potatoes in pan until they are soft and light brown

4. Placed cooked noodles in a bowl and add eggs, spread mixture in skillet to cover completely

5. Place plastic on the skillet and use a pan to press the noodles until they are flatten and condensed. Refrigerate for 25 minutes

6. Remove from refrigerator and set aside on an unlit burner

7. Place another medium pan on medium heat with one (1) tablespoon of olive oil bringing olive oil to a warm

8. Flip contents from the refrigerate pan into the heated pan and fry for ten (10) minutes

9. Set oven to a broil while the sides of the noodles mixture crisp and create a crust

10. Once the sides are fully crispy (this is now the crust) pour the tomato basil sauce on top and leave a little crust out on the edges

11. Top with mozzarella slices, garlic powder, salt and pepper

12. Bake for ten (10) minutes

13. Top with parmesan cheese and basil

14. Slice to preference and grab a slice!

Vegetable Lo-Mein with Broccoli Noodles

Have you tried meatless Mondays? This would be a great dish that both vegans and non-vegans could enjoy.

Servings: 2

Preparation Time: 15 minutes

Ingredients

- 6 Broccoli Florets (2 cups)

- Olive Oil (2 tablespoons)

- Garlic (3 teaspoons, crushed)

- Ginger (2 teaspoons, crushed)

- Cauliflower florets (2 cups)

- Snap Peas (10)

- Green Bell Pepper (2, sliced)

- Bok Choy (2 heads, remove white ends)

- Carrots (1 cup, sliced)

- Red Pepper Flakes (1 teaspoon)

- Sesame Oil (1 tablespoon)

- Vegetable Broth (1/4 cup)

- Soy Sauce (2 tablespoons)

- Hoisin Sauce (2 tablespoons)

- Corn Starch (2 tablespoons)

Directions

1. Place broccoli stems in spiralizer to create noodles

2. In a sauce pan place cauliflower and carrots in fill with enough water to cover vegetables

3. Boil vegetables for five (5) minutes until forking is easy, remove from pan, drain and set aside

4. In a bowl mix the sauce using sesame oil, vegetable broth, soy sauce, hoisin sauce and corn starch until starch is completely incorporated

5. Place olive oil in a medium pan over medium heat and sauté green bell peppers for five (5) minutes, place garlic, ginger, red pepper flakes, carrots, cauliflower, salt and pepper

6. Cook mixture for seven (7) minutes then include broccoli noodles, bok choy and prepare sauce

7. Continue to stir and cook until noodles are completely coated and soft.
8. Plate and enjoy!

Cheese filled Zucchini-Quinoa Casserole

Quick, filling and easy casserole for a fun night in.

Servings: 4

Preparation Time: 40 minutes

Ingredients

- Quinoa (1 1/2 cup, cooked)

- Olive Oil (2 tablespoons)

- Salt (1 teaspoon)

- Black Pepper (1 teaspoon)

- Sharp Cheddar Cheese (7 oz.)

- Large Zucchini (2)

- Parmesan Cheese (2 tablespoons)

Directions

1. Place zucchini in spiralizer and create noodles

2. Set oven to 410 degrees

3. In a bowl place zucchini noodles, sharp cheddar cheese, olive oil, quinoa and season with salt and pepper

4. Spread ingredients in baking dish and top with parmesan cheese

5. Bake for 40 minutes

6. Remove from oven, plate & enjoy

Broccoli Noodles with Avocado Pesto

Go green on your plate and you will feel so much better when you do. Fresh greens aren't only tasty but are good for your body too. Creamy avocado pairs with crunchy broccoli for a tasty meal.

Servings: 4

Preparation Time: 40 minutes

Ingredients

- Large Avocado (2, halved)

- Broccoli Florets (3 cups)

- Tomatoes (2, diced)

- Garlic (4 cloves, crushed)

- Olive Oil (4 teaspoons)

- Lemon Juice (2 tablespoons)

- Salt & Pepper to taste

- Almonds (1/4 cup, to garnish)

Directions

Spiralizer Recipes

1. Place broccoli stems in spiralizer and create noodles

2. Pit garlic, avocado, olive oil, almonds and lemon juice in blender and pulse until smooth.

3. Season with salt and pepper and add pesto to noodles; toss to combine.

4. Plate and top with tomatoes.

Potato Fettuccini with Lime-Garlic glazed Shrimp

Robust garlic and tangy lime coats succulent shrimp and is paired with spiralized potatoes for a filling meal.

Servings: 1

Preparation Time: 30 minutes

Ingredients

- Shrimp (4oz cleaned and deveined)

- Large Potato (1)

- Garlic (2 cloves, minced)

- Grape Tomatoes (10, halved)

- Olive Oil (2 tablespoons)

- Red Pepper Flakes (1 teaspoon)

- Lemon Juice (1/2 tablespoons)

- Salt & Pepper to taste

Directions

1. Place potato in spiralizer, use fettuccini blade to process potatoes.

2. Place medium pan over medium heat, add one tablespoon of olive oil red pepper flakes, half serving of garlic, shrimp, salt and pepper and cook for ten (10) minutes, set cooked shrimp aside

3. In same pan, place other serving of garlic, one tablespoon of olive oil, potato noodles and cook for three (3) minutes

4. Combine the cooked shrimp and tomatoes in the pan, pour lemon juice over noodles.

5. Remove from stove, plate and serve

Butternut Squash Noodles with Potatoes & String Beans

Butternut brings sweetness to this simple dish. It is easy to pull together.

Servings: 1

Preparation Time: 30 minutes

Ingredients

- Butternut Squash (1)

- Large Potato (1, baked & mashed)

- String Beans (1/2 cup)

- Grape Tomatoes (10, halved)

- Large Onion (1, sliced)

- Garlic (2 cloves, crushed)

- Olive Oil (2 tablespoons)

Directions

1. Peel butternut squash, slice in half and remove the middle parts, spiralize the halves into noodles

2. In a medium pan over medium heat place olive oil and butternut squash noodles, cooking for five (5) minutes.

3. Add onions, string beans and garlic to the pan, cook for an additional five (5) minutes

4. Combine mashed potato to mixture, sprinkle olive oil and top with tomatoes

5. Happy Eating!

Three Veggie Noodle mix

This is a great way to combine your veggies for an all-round nutritious meal.

Servings: 4

Preparation Time: 30 minutes

Ingredients

- Zucchini (2)

- Broccoli Florets (2 cups)

- Large Carrots (2, peeled)

- Garlic (2 cloves, crushed)

- Small Onion (1, sliced)

- Olive Oil (2 tablespoons)

- Lemon Juice (1/2 tablespoons)

- Salt & Pepper to taste

Directions

1. Place zucchini, broccoli stems and carrots in spiralizer to create noodles

2. Place medium pan over medium heat, add one tablespoon of olive oil, onions and garlic

3. Place noodles in pan and cook until noodles are soft.

4. Remove from pan and plate, drizzle with olive oil and a pinch of salt and pepper

5. Enjoy!

Onion Spaghetti

Instead of creating onion rings, try a little onion spaghetti

Servings: 2

Preparation Time: 30 minutes

Ingredients

- Large Onions (3)

- Olive Oil (3 cups)

- Garlic (1 clove, crushed)

- Red Bell Pepper (1, halved)

- Green Bell Pepper (1, halved)

- Yellow Bell Pepper (1, halved)

- Salt (2 teaspoons)

- Black Pepper (1 teaspoon)

- Basil (to garnish)

Directions

1. Place onions in spiralizer to create spaghetti

2. Place medium pan over high heat, add bell peppers and cook for five (5) minutes

3. Place onion spaghetti in pan and stir until peppers are fully incorporated in noodles, cook for ten (10) minutes or until onion spaghetti is soft and translucent.

4. Sprinkle salt and pepper

5. Garnish with basil, plate & serve

'As Is' Zucchini Salad with Zesty Lime & Herb dressing

No need for pots or pans, toss this salad together in a bowl, drizzle dressing and you're ready to go.

Servings: 2

Preparation Time: 15 minutes

Ingredients

- Large Zucchini (1)

- Carrots (1/2 cup, sliced)

- Cucumbers (1/2 cup, sliced)

- Bell Pepper (1/2 cup, sliced)

- Tomatoes (1/2 cup sliced)

- Green beans (1/2 cup)

- Mayonnaise (1/4 cup)

- Honey (3 teaspoons)

- Lime Juice (1 tablespoon)

- Dried Basil (1 teaspoon)

- Salt & Pepper to taste

Directions

Salutem Tunnel

1. Place zucchini in spiralizer to create noodles

2. Add sliced vegetables in a bowl with noodles

3. In a bowl mix mayonnaise, honey, lime juice, basil, salt and pepper

4. Combine mixed vegetables and noodles in the dressing, noodles would have a softer texture. Plate & Serve.

Cucumber Fettuccini with Beef Marinara

*Enjoy this Italian inspired dish without the added carbs.
Everyone can enjoy this meal.*

Servings: 4

Preparation Time: 50 minutes

Ingredients

- Water (2 cups)

- Olive Oil (3 tablespoons)

- Tomato Sauce (2 cans, 15oz)

- Medium Onion (1, sliced)

- Garlic (2 cloves, crushed)

- Salt (2 tablespoons)

- Black Pepper (2 tablespoons)

- Dried Basil (2 teaspoons)

- Oregano (2 teaspoons)

- Dried Thyme (1 teaspoon)

- Medium Cucumbers (6)

- Beef (2lbs, cubed)

Directions

Salutem Tunnel

1. Place cucumbers in spiralizer using fettuccini blade to create

2. In a medium pan over high heat, place two tablespoon of olive oil in pot, add onions and garlic to the pan and sauté for two (2) minutes.

3. Place beef in pan and keep stirring for ten (10) minutes and cook for an additional ten (10) minutes

4. In a sauce pan add thyme, oregano, basil, tomato sauce, one teaspoon of salt and pepper
5. Place beef in the sauce pan stir for five (5) minutes, then let it simmer for an additional ten (10) minutes

6. In the pan that was used for the beef, sauté the noodles for ten (10) minutes

7. Remove noodles from pot and plate, pouring the beef marinara sauce on top.

Kale Sweet Potato Caesar Salad with Sweet Corn

Bring a bit of a sweet taste to the dish with these sweet potatoes and sweet corn

Servings: 4

Preparation Time: 55 minutes

Ingredients

- Kale (3 cups, sliced)

- Medium Sweet Potato (2, peeled)

- Sweet Corn (1 can, drained)

- Garlic Powder (2 tablespoons)

- Salt (1 teaspoon)

- Black Pepper (1 teaspoon)

- Almonds (1/4 cup)

- Olive Oil (2 tablespoons)

- Unsweetened Almond Milk (1/4 cup)

- Lemon Juice (1 tablespoon)

- Dijon Mustard (1 tablespoon)

Directions

Salutem Tunnel

1. Place sweet potato in spiralizer to create noodles

2. In a medium pan over medium heat pour one tablespoon of olive oil, when the oil is heated, add the sweet potato noodles, sprinkle with one tablespoon of garlic powder, salt and pepper, place lid on pan and leave to cook for ten (10) minutes

3. Remove from pan and set cooked noodles aside

4. In a blender add, almonds, almond milk, one tablespoon of garlic powder, lemon juice and Dijon mustard, pulsate until mixture is smooth and creamy in texture (create dressing)

5. In the medium pan that the noodles were cooked in, place the kale, season with salt and pepper and stir for five (5) minutes.

6. Add kale to bowl with noodles, add dressing and sprinkle sweet corn on top

7. Toss the salad well before serving.

Spiralized Burger

Burger is a great choice for various occasions but it can get hard to keep this type of meal healthy, try spiralizing your vegetables for your burgers instead. Equally delicious and much healthier.

Servings: 1

Preparation Time: 45 minutes

Ingredients

- Cauliflower Florets (3 cups)

- Garlic Powder (1/2 tablespoon)

- Olive Oil (6 tablespoons)

- Large Egg (1)

- Small Onion (2 sliced pieces)

- Tomato (2 sliced pieces)

- Kales (2 pieces)

- Avocado (1, halved)

- Goat Cheese (1 oz., crumbled)

- Olive Oil Cooking Spray

Directions

Salutem Tunnel

1. Place cauliflower stems in spiralizer to create noodles

2. Place medium pan over medium heat, add one tablespoon of olive oil, once the oil is heated add the noodles, garlic powder, salt and pepper and leave to cook for five (5) minutes

3. Remove noodles from pan and place in a bowl, crack egg in the bowl and coat the noodles evenly.

4. Form noodles into balls and place onto wax paper, place another wax paper on top and flatten.

5. Place pressed patties into the refrigerator for 30 minutes

6. In a bowl mix the goat cheese and half the avocado together.

7. The pan that was used for the noodles, add five (5) additional tablespoons of olive oil and heat thoroughly. Once heated remove the burger patties from the refrigerator and add to hot oil using a thong. Cook until patties are firm.

8. Remove patties from the stove and spread the goat cheese and avocado mixture on both buns add the cauliflower burger patty.

9. Add your additional ingredients before serving, tomato, onions and kale.

10. Enjoy....tasty

Beef Zoodle Soup

Chicken noodle soup may have a contender here. Delicious noodle soup without high carb noodles.

Servings: 6

Preparation Time: 45 minutes

Ingredients

- Large Carrots (2, peeled and sliced)

- Small Onion (1, chopped)

- Zucchini (3)

- Beef (3lbs, cooked and cut in cube pieces)

- Olive Oil (2 1/2 tablespoons)

- Beef Broth (5 cups)

- Garlic (3 cloves, crushed)

- Dried Basil (1 tablespoon)

- Oregano (1 tablespoon)

- Fresh Thyme (1 teaspoon)

- Salt & Pepper to taste

Directions

1. Place zucchini in spiralizer to create noodles and set aside

2. In a large sauce pan over high heat pour in beef broth, onions, garlic, beef bits, oregano, basil, thyme, carrots, salt and pepper.

3. Allow pot to boil for 30 minutes then bring to a simmer and continue to stir for an additional five (5) minutes

4. Place zoodles in a bowl and pour the broth mixture over zoodles. Serve while hot.

Deep-Fried Carrot Curls

You don't have to have fries to enjoy deep fried food.

Servings: 2

Preparation Time: 20 minutes

Ingredients

- Cornstarch (3 tablespoons)

- Olive Oil (4 cups)

- Milk (2 tablespoons)

- All Purpose Flour (3/4 cup)

- Large Egg (1)

- Large Carrot (1, peeled)

Directions

1. Place carrot in spiralizer using the spiral blade

2. In a large sauce pan pour olive oil and bring to a heat

3. Prep two (2) zip lock bags, one bag with egg and milk mixture and the other with flour and cornstarch mixture

4. Take carrot spirals and place in egg mixture bag and shake until spirals are fully coated, take spiral out and add to flour mixture, shake until fully coated

5. Once all spirals are coated with the egg and flour mixture, place in heated olive oil until golden brown

6. Once all spirals are completed pat with paper towel to remove any extra oil, sprinkle with salt and pepper

7. Serve and enjoy!

Onion Omelet

Onions play a major role in this breakfast meal.

Servings: 2

Preparation Time: 25 minutes

Ingredients

- Large Onions (2)

- Large Eggs (2)

- Milk (1/2 cup)

- Fresh Cilantro (3 tablespoons)

- Spinach (1/2 cup)

- Butter (2 tablespoons)

- Mozzarella Cheese (4 tablespoons)

- Salt (1 teaspoon)

- Black Pepper (1 teaspoon)

Directions

1. Place onions in spiralizer to create noodles

2. In a medium pan over high heat, add onion noodles, spinach and cilantro and cook until onions are translucent and tender. Ensure the onion noodles are fully covered in the pan.

3. In a bowl mix eggs and milk and pour in pan to cover noodles, cook for an additional seven (7) minutes. Sprinkle mozzarella cheese, salt and pepper over omelet

4. Fold, slice and serve the omelet for two.

Greek Cucumber Salad

Have a light, refreshing salad with a touch of Greece

Servings: 4

Preparation Time: 25 minutes

Ingredients

- Olive Oil (3 tablespoons)
- Lime Juice (2 tablespoons)
- Onion (1, sliced)
- Kalamata pitted olives (12, sliced)
- Cherry Tomatoes (12, sliced)
- Zucchini (1/4, sliced)
- Cucumber (2)
- Oregano (1 tablespoon)
- Fresh Thyme (1 tablespoon)
- Feta Cheese (2 oz.)
- Salt (1 teaspoon)
- Black Pepper (1 teaspoon)

Directions

Salutem Tunnel

1. Place cucumbers in spiralizer to create noodles

2. In a bowl add created cucumber noodles, zucchini, tomatoes, olives, onion slices and feta cheese

3. In a separate bowl combine olive oil, lime juice, salt, oregano, thyme and pepper and mix until smooth texture

4. Pour over create noodles and toss until all noodles are fully coated, place in refrigerator for 15 minutes

5. Remove and serve chilled

Potato Alfredo

Potato noodles coated in a creamy Alfredo sauce is a spin on traditional Alfredo.

Servings: 4

Preparation Time: 30 minutes

Ingredients

- Potatoes (4)

- Mushrooms (8 oz.)

- String Beans (1 cup, sliced)

- Mozzarella (2 oz.)

- Olive Oil (3 tablespoons)

- Alfredo Sauce (1 cup- brand of your choose)

- Cherry Tomatoes (12, sliced)

- Cinnamon (1 pinch)

- Salt, Pepper & Basil to taste

Directions

1. Place potatoes in spiralizer to create noodles and boil for ten (10) minutes

2. In a medium pan over high heat, pour olive oil and bring to a heat, sauté mushrooms, string beans and mozzarella for five (5) minutes

3. Pour Alfredo sauce, potatoes in the mixture, mix gently and let it sit for four (4) minutes, add cherry tomatoes and remove pan from heat.

4. Plate noodles topped with cinnamon, basil, salt and pepper.

Grilled Chicken with Zucchini Noodles

Grilled chicken helps to complete a fresh and crunchy salad that's great for lunch or dinner.

Servings: 5

Preparation Time: 15 minutes

Ingredients

- Zucchini (6)

- Chicken Breast (1lb, grilled & sliced)

- Olive Oil (10 tablespoons)

- Red wine vinegar (2 tablespoons)

- Lemon Juice (1 teaspoon)

- Fresh Basil (4 tablespoons, chopped)

- Toasted Nuts (1/4 cup)

- Garlic (2 cloves, crushed)

- Red Pepper Flakes (1 tablespoon)

- Salt (1 teaspoon)

- Black Pepper (1 teaspoon)

Directions

Salutem Tunnel

1. Place zucchini in spiralizer to create zoodles and set aside

2. In a blender, create dressing by mixing 5 tablespoons of olive oil, nuts, red wine vinegar, lemon juice and red pepper flakes and blend until smooth texture.

3. Place zoodles in a pan over low heat and sauté until zoodles are soft, pour three (3) tablespoons of the dressing on zoodles and toss until fully covered with dressing.

4. Remove from pan, plate and top with grilled chicken slices and sprinkle salt and pepper, add more dressing if you wish. Enjoy!

Crispy Shrimp Zucchini Noodle Wrap

Easy snack to make and take on the go you have so you don't miss a meal or it can help you to avoid greasy junk food.

Servings: 1

Preparation Time: 15 minutes

Ingredients

- Whole Grain Tortilla (1)

- Zucchini (1/2)

- Carrot (1/2)

- Shrimp (2lbs, deveined & cleaned)

- Black Beans (4 tablespoons)

- Hummus (3 tablespoons- brand of your choose)

- Olive Oil (2 tablespoons)

- Avocado (1/2, insides sliced)

- Feta Cheese (4 tablespoons)

- Garlic (2 cloves, crushed)

- Salt (1 teaspoon)

- Black Pepper (1 teaspoon)

Directions

Salutem Tunnel

1. Place zucchini in spiralizer to create noodles

2. In a medium pan over medium, add olive oil, heat and
   sauté the shrimp with salt, pepper and garlic. Cook until
   shrimp is golden brown.

3. Place the wrap on a plate and cover with hummus, add
   crispy shrimp, avocado slices, carrots, beans, zoodles
   and sprinkle with feta cheese.

4. Roll the wrap and secure with toothpicks. Enjoy!

Shrimp Broccoli Noodles with Feta Cheese

Shrimp and Feta Cheese equals greatness

Servings: 2

Preparation Time: 20 minutes

Ingredients

- Shrimp (2lbs, deveined and cleaned)

- Broccoli (10 florets, rinsed)

- Garlic (2 cloves, minced)

- Lemon Juice (1 teaspoon)

- Red Pepper Flakes (1 teaspoon)

- Feta Cheese (6 cubes)

Directions

1. Place broccoli stems in spiralizer to create noodles and set aside

2. In a medium pan over high heat, spray pan with cooking spray, add shrimp, garlic, salt and pepper and sauté for ten (10) minutes

3. In the same pan, reduce the heat and pour in lemon juice and broccoli noodles, let it cook for five (5) minutes

4. Remove from pan and plate, sprinkle red pepper flakes and crumble feta cheese. Enjoy

Sweet Potato Noodles with crispy bacon

Bacon makes everything okay and these potato noodles will surely tell the tale.

Servings: 2

Preparation Time: 35 minutes

Ingredients

- Bacon (6 strips)

- Sweet Potatoes (2, peeled)

- Olive Oil (2 tablespoons)

- Garlic (1 clove, crushed)

- Red Pepper Flakes (1 tablespoon)

- Beef Broth (1/2 cup)

- Fresh Parsley (2 tablespoons, sliced)

- Salt & Pepper taste

Directions

1. Place sweet potato in spiralizer to create noodles

2. In a medium skillet over medium heat, stir fry the bacon strips until very crispy, remove from pan and let cool, once cooled, crumble into bits

3. In the same skillet place the sweet potato noodles along with garlic, red pepper flakes, salt and pepper, stir for five (5) minutes

4. Pour in beef broth and add parsley, leave to cook for an additional ten (10) minutes

5. Remove from pan and plate noodles, sprinkle with bacon bits and serve

Bell Pepper Chicken Parmesan

Colorful Parmesan bell pepper mix is simple and delicious.

Servings: 4

Preparation Time: 30 minutes

Ingredients

- Wheat Breadcrumbs (1/2 cup)

- Parmesan Cheese (1/2 cup)

- Italian Herbs (1 tablespoon- brand of your choose)

- Olive Oil (2 tablespoons)

- Chicken Breasts (4)

- Tomato Sauce (2 cups- brand of your choose)

- Mozzarella Cheese (4 slices)

- Green, Red and Yellow Bell Peppers (1/2 of each, halved & seeds removed)

- Fresh Basil (1 teaspoon)

Directions

1. Place bell peppers in spiralizer to create noodles

2. Set oven at 430 degrees

3. In a bowl, mix breadcrumbs, parmesan, Italian herbs, salt and pepper. Coated chicken breast pieces fully with bread crumbs

4. In a medium pan over high heat, add olive oil and allow to heat. Place coated chicken breast in pan cook for five (5) minutes on both sides

5. Lift pan and place in oven for ten (10) minutes, remove pan and pour in tomato sauce and top with mozzarella slices allow to cook for an additional five (5) minutes.

6. Plate the raw bell peppers and place chicken on top with more parmesan and basil

Apple Spinach Salad with cheese

Sweet, Savory.....Salad!

Serving: 1

Preparation Time: 10 minutes

Ingredients:

- Spinach (1 package)
- Large Apple (1)
- Dried Cranberries (1/4 cup)
- Goat Cheese (1/3 cup, crumbled)
- Nuts (1/4 cup- brand of your choose)

Directions:

1. Place apple in spiralizer to create noodles
2. In a bowl, add spinach, apple noodles, cranberries with a pinch of salt
3. Garnish with cheese, nuts and dressing of choice.

BBQ Zucchini Bowl

Bountiful Bowl!

Servings: 3

Preparation Time: 30 minutes

Ingredients:

- Zucchini (3)
- Broccoli Florets (6, sliced)
- Large Carrots (2, grated)
- Purple cabbage (1.5 cups, grated)
- Mushrooms (8, sliced)
- BBQ (1 cup, homemade or store bought)
- Onion (1/2 cup, chopped)
- Garlic (2 cloves, diced)
- Avocado (1/2, sliced)
- Salt & Pepper to taste

Directions:

1. Place zucchini in spiralizer to create zoodles

2. Cook onions and garlic over in a medium pan over medium heat for three (3) minutes

3. Add sliced broccoli, grated carrots and sliced mushrooms to pan and cook for ten (10) minutes

4. Pour in BBQ sauce and leave to simmer for an additional four (4) minutes

5. Plate zoodles and pour vegetable mix on top, garnish with avocado slices and Enjoy!

Butternut crème sauce over Zucchini fettuccini

Full flavor for the health conscious!

Serving: 6

Preparation Time: 70 minutes

Ingredients:

- Butternut squash (1)
- Olive oil (2 tablespoons)
- Sweet Onion (1, chopped)
- Garlic (2 cloves ,diced)
- Coconut milk (1 cup)
- Salt (1 tablespoon)
- Mushrooms (dozen, chopped)
- Zucchini (3)

Directions:

1. Place zucchini in spiralizer to create zoodles
2. Heat oven to 375 degrees
3. Cut squash in half along length, cover baking sheet with olive oil-(cut side down) place squash on baking sheet.

4. Let sit in oven for 40 minutes, allow cooling time after baking, remove skin and add remaining squash to blender.

5. Begin sautéing onions, garlic in a tablespoon of olive oil over medium heat for about four (4) minutes

6. Blend garlic, onions, coconut milk, salt and squash until creamy.

7. Sauté mushrooms until browning occurs, add noodles and cook for four (4) minutes until tender, add sauce and allow cook for an additional four (4) minutes

8. Add freshly ground black pepper for finishing touch.

9. ENJOY!

Ground beef sweet potato casserole

Savory goodness...

Servings: 4

Preparation Time: 55 minutes

Ingredients:

- Olive Oil (1 tablespoon)
- Small Onion (½ chopped)
- Green Bell Pepper (1, chopped)
- Ground Beef (1 lb., thinly sliced)
- Oregano (1 teaspoon)
- Parsley (1 teaspoon)
- Basil (2 tablespoons, diced)
- Can Tomatoes (1)
- Medium Potatoes (2)
- Cheddar Cheese (8 oz.)

Directions

1. Set oven to 350 degrees.
2. Add olive oil to pan over medium heat.

3. Cook onions and bell peppers for five (5) minutes, mix in garlic and continue to mix for two (2) minutes

4. Place the ground beef in the pan and allow to cook until browning occurs.

5. Add parsley, oregano, tomatoes and basil.

6. Lower heat and allow to cook for an additional 20 minutes.

7. Place potatoes in spiralizer to create noodles once completed, mix in with beef.

8. Allow to cook for a further six (6) minutes.

9. Pour mixture in casserole dish, cover and bake in oven for 20 minutes

10. Uncover, plate and indulge

Mandarin and mint salad w/ spiralized beets

Sweet mandarin with fresh mint is combined with bright beets.

Serving: 4

Preparation: 30 minutes

Ingredients:

- Mandarin oranges (8 oz., in juice)
- Olive Oil (2 tablespoons)
- Red Wine Vinegar (2 tablespoons)
- Beets (2, snip ends)
- Mint leaves (1 bunch)

Directions:

1. Place beets in spiralizer to create noodles
2. Squeeze liquid from oranges into tablespoons (keep 2 tablespoons for later use)
3. Mix mandarin juice, olive oil and red wine vinegar.
4. Stir beets in with mixture.
5. Plate, garnish with mint leaves and enjoy!

Spiral Apple Tart

Sweet treat for any day of the week!

Servings: 3

Preparation Time: 15 minutes

Ingredients:

- Dried Apples (1 cup, slices)
- Pitted Dates (1/2 cup)
- Cinnamon (2 teaspoons)
- Large Apple (1)
- Brown Sugar (2 tablespoons)
- Cinnamon (1 teaspoons)

Directions:

1. Cut dried apples into small pieces. Place dates, dried apples and cinnamon in blender and blend until smooth.
2. Form dough from blender mixture into muffin tins (be sure to place baking cups in tin).
3. Place dough in fridge for 40 minutes
4. Place apples in spiralizer to create noodles, mix with sugar and cinnamon.
5. Let sit in fridge overnight.
6. Place apple noodles mixture on dough.

7. Enjoy!

Spiralized Apples atop cinnamon and Yogurt

A fun, simple, yummy treat for all!

Servings: 2

Preparation time: 20 minutes

Ingredients:

- Medium Apple (1)
- Lemon Juice (1 teaspoon)
- Pecans (1 tablespoon, diced)
- Oats (2 teaspoons)
- Butter (1 teaspoon)
- Ground Cinnamon (1 teaspoon)
- Brown sugar (2 teaspoons)
- Yogurt of choice (8 ounces)

Directions:

1. Place apples in spiralizer and create noodles
2. Set pan to medium heat, add pecans and oats to pan until slightly toasted
3. Add butter to pan, 1/4 teaspoon brown sugar and cinnamon.

4. Turn heat off, mix remainder of cinnamon with yogurt, garnish with apple noodles.
5. Serve and enjoy!

Spicy Mexican Style Noodles

Feeling for a difference, travel to Mexico via your dish.
A mouthful of Mexican flavors will tantalize your palate.

Servings: 1

Preparation time: 15 minutes

Ingredients:

- Large Carrot (1)
- Zucchini (1)
- Cucumber (1)
- Hot Sauce (2 tablespoons- brand of your choice)
- Olive Oil (4 tablespoons)
- Garlic (1 clove, crushed)
- Jalapeno (1/2, sliced)
- Oregano (1 teaspoon)
- Tomato sauce (4 tablespoons- brand of your choice)
- Paprika (1 teaspoon)
- Turmeric (1 teaspoon)
- Salt (2 teaspoons)
- Black Pepper (2 teaspoons)
- Fresh Thyme (for garnish)

Directions:

Salutem Tunnel

1. Place carrot, zucchini and cucumber in spiralizer and create noodles
2. Set pan to medium heat, add olive oil and bring to a heat, stir garlic, jalapeno, oregano, paprika, turmeric, salt and pepper in pan and cook for five (5) minutes
3. Slowly pour in tomato sauce and hot sauce, continue to stir for two (2) minutes
4. Add noodles to pan and cook until soften
5. Turn heat off, mix plate noodles and add fresh to thyme to garnish

Fried Chicken with Potato Spirals

Everyone loves fry chicken; you don't have to have it with regular chips have it with potato spirals!

Servings: 2

Preparation time: 40 minutes

Ingredients:

- Chicken Legs (4)
- Breadcrumbs (1/2 cup)
- Cornstarch (6 tablespoons)
- Large Egg (1)
- Milk (1/2 cup)
- Potatoes (4, peeled)
- Olive Oil (1 cup)
- Garlic Powder (1 tablespoon)
- Paprika (1 teaspoon)
- Salt (1 teaspoon)
- Black Pepper (1 teaspoon)

Directions:

1. Place potatoes in spiralizer, choose the correct blade to create spirals

2. In a small bowl combine breadcrumbs, garlic powder, paprika, cornstarch, salt and pepper and in another small bowl combine egg and milk

3. In a medium skillet over medium heat bring olive oil to heat until bubbling

4. Place chicken legs in egg mixture, coat completely, remove chicken legs and place in breadcrumbs mixture, coat completely.

5. Slowly place chicken legs in pan and fry for 15 minutes on both sides

6. In the same pan, deep fry potato spirals until golden brown

7. Plate chicken legs and potato spirals, serve and enjoy!

Grilled Salmon with Red Onion Noodles

Tangy grilled salmon topped with juicy red onion noodles

Servings: 2

Preparation time: 30 minutes

Ingredients:

- Salmon (2 fillet, grilled)
- Red Onions (4)
- Lemon Juice (4 tablespoons)
- Olive Oil (2 tablespoons)
- Red Wine Vinegar (1 tablespoon)
- Basil (1 teaspoon)
- Dried Thyme (1 teaspoon)
- Salt & Pepper to taste

Directions:

1. Place red onions in spiralizer and create noodles
2. Set medium skillet to medium heat, add olive oil and bring to heat
3. In a bowl, mix lemon juice, red wine vinegar, basil, thyme, salt and pepper

4. Sauté red onion noodles in pan for five (5) minutes then remove from heat
5. Plate noodles and add grilled salmon on top, drizzle with lemon juice mixture
6. Serve and enjoy!

Pear Arugula Salad with Feta Cheese

So simple and filling, quick and easy, try!

Servings: 1

Preparation time: 10 minutes

Ingredients:

- Arugula (1 bunch)
- Large Pear (1)
- Dried Cranberries (3 tablespoons)
- Feta Cheese (1/4 cup, crumbled)
- Almonds (1/4 cup)
- Dressing of choice
- Pinch of salt

Directions:

1. In a bowl, place arugula, cranberries and salt and combine thoroughly
2. Place pear in spiralizer to create noodles and add the noodles to the bowl
3. Combine ingredients thoroughly and crumble cheese and almonds on top
4. Plate and serve with dressing of choice

Pesto Carrots with Tomatoes

A unique dish with a great taste

Servings: 2

Preparation time: 15 minutes

Ingredients:

- Medium Carrots (2)
- Quinoa (1/4 cup, already cooked & drained)
- Tomatoes (2, chopped)
- Pesto Sauce (brand of your choice)
- Almonds (2 tablespoons)

Directions:

1. Place carrots in spiralizer to create noodles
2. In a bowl combine carrot noodles with cooked quinoa, pesto sauce and chopped tomatoes
3. Top with almonds and serve

Sweet Potato & Carrot Lo- Mein

Chinese dish with a twirl.

Servings: 4

Preparation time: 40 minutes

Ingredients:

- Olive Oil (2 teaspoons)
- Green Onions (2, sliced)
- Garlic (1 clove, crushed)
- Soy Sauce (6 tablespoons)
- Cornstarch (2 tablespoons)
- Ginger (1 tablespoon, grated)
- Medium Carrots (3, peeled)
- Sweet Potatoes (3)
- Grilled Chicken (1 cup, grilled and sliced)
- Roasted Almonds (to garnish)

Directions:

1. In a medium pan over medium heat pour olive oil and bring to heat
2. Place green onions and garlic in pan, stir for five (5) minutes

3. In a small bowl, mix soy sauce, cornstarch and ginger
4. Place the sweet potatoes and carrots in spiralizer to create noodles
5. Add noodles to pan along with sauce and stir for ten (10) minutes, thereafter add grilled chicken slices
6. Remove from pan, plate and serve

Cheesy Cheese Noodles

Fun snack for all cheese lovers and persons willing to indulge

Servings: 1

Preparation time: 5 minutes

Ingredients:

- Parmesan Cheese (1 teaspoon)
- Pecorino (1lb,chilled)
- Cheddar Cheese (1lb,chilled)
- Olive Oil (1 teaspoon)
- Salt & Pepper to taste

Directions:

1. Place chilled cheese in spiralizer and create noodles
2. Plate and drizzle with olive oil, salt and pepper.
3. Top with Parmesan and serve!

Peas & Pesto Cucumber Noodles

Go green.....a color that always brings your dish to life

Servings: 4

Preparation time: 40 minutes

Ingredients:

- Olive Oil (5 tablespoons)
- Cucumber (2)
- Green Peas (1 can)
- Almonds (2 tablespoons)
- Basil (2 cups)
- Parmesan cheese (2 tablespoons)
- Garlic (1 clove, crushed)
- Salt & Pepper to taste

Directions:

1. Place cucumber in spiralizer and create noodles
2. In a large pan over high heat pour in 2 tablespoons of olive oil and sauté noodles for ten (10) minutes. Remove from pan and set aside to cool

3. In a blender add, almonds, basil, parmesan cheese, 3 tablespoons of olive oil, garlic, salt and pepper and blend until smooth, creamy texture

4. Plate noodles and pour mixture from blend, sprinkle with green peas

5. Serve & Enjoy

Cantaloupe Noodles with Lemon Juice

This soft fruit makes for succulent noodles

Servings: 2

Preparation time: 10 minutes

Ingredients:

- Cantaloupes (3, removed from skin, sliced)
- Honeydew (3, removed from skin, sliced)
- Lemon Juice (6 tablespoons)
- Almonds (1/2 cup)
- Fresh Mint to Garnish

Directions:

1. Place cantaloupe and honeydew in spiralizer and create noodles
2. Place noodles in a bowl, pour lemon juice and sprinkle with almonds, toss so all ingredients are fully incorporated
3. Plate and top with fresh mint. Enjoy!

Sweet and Sour Pear Noodles

Pear may not be your first thought when it comes to sweet and sour but this dish will not disappoint.

Servings: 2

Preparation time: 10 minutes

Ingredients:

- Pear (6)
- Oranges (2, squeezed)
- Lemon Zest (1 teaspoon)
- Grapes (seedless, sliced)
- Mint leaves to garnish

Directions:

1. Place pear in spiralizer and create noodles
2. Place noodles in a bowl along with sliced grapes, squeeze orange on top and sprinkle with lemon zest
3. Toss to fully incorporate ingredients
4. Garnish with mint leaves and serve.

Zesty Cabbage Noodle Salad with Ginger & lime Vinaigrette

Crunchy cabbage infused with citrus and earthy ginger.

Servings: 2

Preparation time: 25 minutes

Ingredients:

- Cabbage (2 heads, sliced)
- Cucumber (1/2 sliced)
- Ginger (2 tablespoons, grated)
- Lime Juice (1/4 cup)
- Olive Oil (2 tablespoons)
- Brown Sugar (2 tablespoons)
- Salt (Pinch)

Directions:

1. Place cabbage in spiralizer to create noodles
2. In a medium skillet on low heat, add olive oil and cabbage, sauté for five (5) minutes
3. Add ginger, lime juice, brown sugar and salt to the pan and allow to cook for two (2) minutes

4. Plate cabbage noodles, top with thinly sliced cucumbers.

Carrot & Beets Noodles with Applesauce and Feta Cheese

Nothing beats a mixture of fruits and vegetables and what a fun way to have it......Noodles

Servings: 3

Preparation time: 20 minutes

Ingredients:

- Large Carrots (2, peeled)
- Beets (2, sliced)
- Applesauce (4 tablespoons- homemade or store bought)
- Feta Cheese (1/4 cup, crumbled)
- Water (5 cups)
- Olive Oil (2 tablespoons)
- Basil (1 teaspoon)

Directions:

1. Place carrots and beets in spiralizer to create noodles
2. In a sauce pan bring five (5) cups of water to a boil, place noodles in boiling water and cook for five (5) minutes

3. Remove and drain noodles

4. In a bowl, mix basil, olive oil and applesauce

5. Combine noodles with mixture

6. Plate and serve with feta cheese on top. Enjoy!

Crispy Apple Fettuccini with Bacon Strips

What better what to enjoy apples than with bacon?

Servings: 3

Preparation time: 20 minutes

Ingredients:

- Large Apples (5)
- Bacon (4 strips)
- Olive Oil (1 cup)
- Garlic (1 clove, crushed)
- Brown Sugar (1 tablespoon)
- Salt (1 teaspoon)
- Black Pepper (1 teaspoon)

Directions:

1. Place apples in spiralizer using fettuccini blade
2. In a medium pan on high heat, pour olive oil and stir in garlic. Fry bacon strips until extremely crispy, sprinkle with salt and pepper
3. Let bacon strips cool before using hands to crumble strips into bits

4. Toss Apple fettuccini in same pan and fry for two (2) minutes

5. Remove from pan and sprinkle with brown sugar

6. Plate and top with bacon bits. Enjoy!

Stir Fry Sweet Potato Noodles with Beef Stripes

No better way to enjoy beef than with sweet potatoes

Servings: 2

Preparation time: 40 minutes

Ingredients:

- Sweet Potatoes (6, peeled)
- Beef (2lbs, sliced in stripes)
- Olive Oil (4 tablespoons)
- Garlic (2 cloves, crushed)
- Red Pepper Flakes (1 teaspoon)
- Paprika (1 tablespoon)
- Oregano (1 teaspoon)
- Fresh Thyme (1 teaspoon)
- Beef Broth (1/2 cup)
- Cherry Tomatoes (12, halved)
- Lemon Juice (1 teaspoon)

Directions:

1. Place sweet potatoes in spiralizer to create noodles

2. In a pan on high heat, with olive oil, place garlic, red pepper flakes, paprika, oregano, thyme, sauté for two (2) minutes

3. Add beef stripes and cook on both sides for ten (10) minutes each

4. Pour beef broth in pan and lower heat, let contents simmer for five (5) minutes

5. Remove beef stripes and sauté noodles in the same pan for three (3) minutes

6. Remove from pan and plate noodles with beef stripes on top

7. Place tomato cherries on top and drizzle lemon juice.

Chili Con Carne with Carrot Noodles

Whoever said that chili has to be eaten with rice?

Servings: 2

Preparation time: 30 minutes

Ingredients:

- Black Beans (1 can)
- Medium Carrots (4, peeled)
- Italian Sausage (2lbs, minced)\
- Olive Oil (3 tablespoons)
- Tomato Sauce (1 can- brand of your choice)
- Tomato (1, sliced)
- Basil (1 teaspoon)
- Oregano (1 teaspoon)
- Thyme (1 tablespoon)
- Italian herbs (2 tablespoons- brand of your choice)
- Salt & Pepper to taste

Directions:

1. Place carrots in spiralizer and create noodles

2. In a medium skillet, pour olive oil in pan and stir fry sausage for 15 minutes

3. Add Tomato Sauce, sliced tomato, basil, oregano, thyme, Italian herbs, salt and pepper to the pan and let simmer for seven (7) minutes

4. Add black beans and leave to simmer for another five (5) minutes

5. Plate carrots noodles and pour chili mixture from pan

6. Serve & Enjoy!

Cheesy Zucchini Pasta

Just like the good old mac n cheese without the high carb noodles.

Servings: 4

Preparation time: 15 minutes

Ingredients:

- Zucchini (4)
- Cheddar Cheese (4 cups)
- Milk (1 cup)
- Olive Oil (2 tablespoons)
- Salt & Pepper to taste

Directions:

1. Spiralize the zucchini to create noodles
2. In a sauce pan add milk, cheddar cheese, olive oil, salt and pepper, let the mixture cook for ten (10) minutes on low heat
3. Add zoodles to pan and let simmer for five (5) minutes
4. Serve this creamy dish and enjoy.

Ginger-Scallion Shrimp and Cucumber Noodles

The scallion and ginger flavor the shrimp to accompany fresh cucumber noodles.

Servings: 2

Preparation time: 25 minutes

Ingredients:

- Shrimp (2lbs, deveined and cleaned)
- Ginger (1/4 cup, grated)
- Green Onions (1, chopped)
- Cucumber (2)
- Garlic Powder (1 teaspoon)
- Lime Juice (1 teaspoon)
- Salt (1 teaspoon)
- Black Pepper (1 teaspoon)
- Cooking Spray

Directions:

1. Spiralize cucumber and create noodles
2. In a medium pan over high heat, sprayed with cooking spray sauté shrimp with garlic powder and ginger for 15 minutes

3. Remove shrimp and sauté noodles in the same pan with lime juice, salt and pepper, for an additional five (5) minutes

4. Remove noodles and plate, top with shrimp and sprinkle with green onions.

Spicy Tuna Bell Pepper Noodles with Sweet Corn

Bell Pepper serves a greater purpose that just to season a few of our meals, they serve as filling noodles when eaten as a main dish.

Servings: 2

Preparation time: 25 minutes

Ingredients:

- Yellow Bell Pepper (2)
- Tuna (1 can- brand of your choice)
- Hot Sauce (2 tablespoons)
- Sweet Corn (1 can)
- Paprika (1 tablespoon)
- Olive Oil (2 tablespoons)
- Oregano (1 teaspoon)
- Salt & Pepper to taste

Directions:

1. Spiralize yellow bell peppers to create jagged noodles
2. In a medium pan, pour in olive oil and bring pan to medium heat
3. Sauté tuna along with hot sauce, paprika and oregano

4. Combine jagged noodles with sauce in pan
5. Plate mixture and sprinkle with sweet corn
6. Enjoy!

Spicy Chickpeas with Veggie Noodles

*Chickpeas can make for a very filling meal. Red pepper
and curry add much spice to this healthy meal.*

Servings: 3

Preparation time: 15 minutes

Ingredients:

- Cabbage (1 cup)
- Yellow Bell Pepper (3, sliced)
- Large Carrots (2, peeled)
- Large Cucumbers (2)
- Garlic (1 clove, crushed)
- Cilantro (2 tablespoons, diced)
- Chickpeas (1 can, washed & drained)
- Red Pepper Flakes (1 teaspoon)
- Salt (1 teaspoon)
- Black Pepper (1 teaspoon)
- Nut Butter (2 tablespoons)
- Lime Juice (2 tablespoons)
- Maple Syrup (4 tablespoons)
- Curry Powder (1 tablespoon)
- Ginger (1 tablespoon, grated)
- Water (1 cup)

Directions:

1. In a bowl, mix water, ginger, curry powder, maple syrup, lime juice and butter
2. Place bell peppers, carrots and cucumbers in spiralizer to create noodles
3. Add cabbage and veggie noodles to bowl mixture and toss so everything is well coated
4. Add chickpeas and continue to mix until everything is fully incorporated
5. Serve & Enjoy!

Vegan gluten-free veggie noodles

A fun and simple vegetarian dish that anyone can enjoy and it's ready in less than 30 minutes.

Servings: 3

Preparation time: 15 minutes

Ingredients:

- Large Cucumber (3)
- Sweet Potatoes (3)
- Green Onion (3, sliced)
- Cabbage (1 cup, sliced)

- Broccoli Florets (1 cup)
- Nuts (1/2 cup, minced)
- Cilantro (1/2 cup, sliced)
- Almond Butter (2 tablespoons)
- Maple Syrup (3 tablespoons)
- Lime Juice (3 tablespoons)
- Garlic (1 clove, crushed)
- Ginger (2 teaspoons, grated)

Directions:

1. Use spiralizer to create noodles using potatoes, cucumber and carrots.
2. Place potato spirals along with broccoli onto a baking sheet. Bake at 400 degrees for 10 minutes or until crisp.
3. In a bowl, mix almond butter, maple syrup, lime juice, garlic and ginger
4. Place carrot and cucumber noodles along with cabbage in bowl with mixture and toss to fully incorporate all ingredients except baked veggies.
5. Refrigerate mixture until chilled or for one (1) day for best taste.
6. Add baked vegetables right before serving.
7. Enjoy!

Creamy Almond Spinach & Sweet Corn

Nutty almond combines with fresh spinach and sweet corn for a creamy dish you can enjoy as an appetizer or main dish.

Servings: 2

Preparation time: 40 minutes

Ingredients:

- Almonds (1/2 cup)
- Warm Water (1 cup)
- Vegetable Broth (1 cup)
- Garlic (1 clove, crushed)
- Medium Onion (1, sliced)
- Large Carrot (1, peeled)
- Sweet Corn (1 can)
- Spinach (1 bunch)
- Red Pepper Flakes (2 teaspoons)
- Salt & Pepper to taste
- Cooking Spray

Directions:

1. In a blender add almonds, vegetable broth and garlic, blend until smooth texture is achieved

2. Place carrot and onion in spiralizer to create noodles

3. In a large pan over medium heat spray with cooking spray and sauté carrot and onion noodles for five (5) minutes until onions are translucent.

4. Add sweet corn and spinach with 4 tablespoons of water, cover the pan with lid and allow to simmer for three (3) minutes

5. Add the mixture from blender to the pan, sprinkle with red pepper flakes, salt and black pepper and leave the lid off and cook for two (2) minutes

6. Serve & Enjoy!

Zoodles with Pineapple Bits

Add a little extra sweetness to your dishes with pineapple; get a little taste of the tropics with this dish.

Servings: 2

Preparation time: 20 minutes

Ingredients:

- Zucchini (2)
- Pineapple (6 slices, chopped)
- Lemon Juice (1 teaspoon)
- Coconut (1 cup, shredded)
- Salt to taste

Directions:

1. Spiralize the zucchini to create noodles/zoodles
2. In a bowl add, pineapples bits, lemon juice and salt, mix thoroughly
3. Plate raw zoodles and pour pineapple mixture on top.
4. Add shredded coconut, serve and enjoy!

Carrot Nutmeg Pudding

Nutmeg adds much flavor to this simple dish.

Servings: 2

Preparation time: 20 minutes

Ingredients:

- Large Carrots (2)
- Olive Oil (2 tablespoons)
- Honey (2 1/2 teaspoons)
- Nutmeg (3 teaspoons)
- Raisins (1 tablespoon)

Directions:

1. Spiralize carrots and create noodles
2. Sauté carrots in medium pan over medium heat in one (1) tablespoon of olive oil for five (5) minutes, reduce heat and leave to simmer
3. In a bowl whisk one (1) tablespoon of olive oil, honey and nutmeg
4. Stir this mixture on small pan over low heat for two (2) minutes (do not burn)

5. Remove sauce mixture and pour in pan with carrot noodle, toss the noodles around in sauce so it is fully coated, leave to cook for three (3) minutes
6. Serve warm, topped with raisins.

Description

Do you want to put your spiralizer to use? How would you like to make a wide variety of dishes using your spiralizer? Are you interested in getting your hands on 90+ amazing recipes that you can spiralize? Look no further because you have just found the most fantastic cookbook that you could ever get your hands on!

This cookbook is bound to keep your spiralizer busy and will keep you wanting to make more. Spiralizing your food can really help to turn ordinary dishes into eye-catching creations that are delicious and this spiralizer cookbook will show you exactly how. If you are keen on healthy eating, there is no better way to make sure you eat those veggies than by turning them into spirals, noodles and ribbons.

Imagine preparing from breakfast to dessert with your spiralizer. You can prepare from pancakes to pudding and even pizza-yum. Healthy eating just got a whole lot better and you can join in on the deliciousness with all 90+ recipes included in this spiralizer cookbook. Grab your copy now and you won't be disappointed!

Finally, if you enjoyed this book, then I'd like to ask you for a favor, would you be kind enough to leave a review for this book on Amazon? It'd be greatly appreciated!

Thank you and good luck!

Made in the USA
Las Vegas, NV
28 January 2021

16286164R10079